Official Team GB and ParalympicsGB

Heroes

TEAM GB

ParalympicsGB

Contents

Written by Bronagh Woods

First published by Carlton Books Limited in 2012
Copyright © 2012 Carlton Books Limited

Team GB Lion's head logo TM © British Olympic Association 2009.
ParalympicsGB Lion's head logo TM © BPA 2005–2010.
All rights reserved.

TEAM GB   ParalympicsGB

Carlton Books Limited
20 Mortimer Street, London W1T 3JW

ISBN 978-1-84732-930-1
Printed in China

Official Licensed Team Product

A CIP catalogue record for this book is available from the British Library.

MIX
Paper from
responsible sources
FSC® C101537

Please remember to recycle this book when you have finished enjoying it.

Introduction

On 27 July, a spectacular Opening Ceremony will get the London 2012 Olympic Games under way. The Olympic Games is followed by the Paralympic Games, which has its own Opening Ceremony on 29 August. Team GB athletes will compete at the Olympic Games and ParalympicsGB athletes will compete at the Paralympic Games. In total, British athletes will take part in 46 sports – 26 for the Olympians and 20 for the Paralympians – against challengers from all over the world.

The members of Team GB and ParalympicsGB come from all corners of the UK. Some have already been to previous Olympic or Paralympic Games, while others are just starting out. The one thing they all share is an incredible desire to take a place on the winner's podium.

British Paralympians had their best result ever at the Beijing 2008 Paralympic Games, while Team GB's Olympians achieved their best result for 100 years in the Olympic Games. The last time the Olympians did so well was 1908 – the first time the Games were held in London.

All teams have their heroes and many of the athletes in this book are already the best in the world. Yet the magic of the Games means that there will be many surprises. By 9 September, when the Closing Ceremony of the Paralympic Games marks the end of London 2012, many more British athletes will be famous. Their achievements will inspire a new generation for the next Games at Rio 2016 in Brazil and beyond.

Danielle Brown
Paralympic Archery

ParalympicsGB

Born: 10 April 1988 in Lothersdale, North Yorkshire
Event: Individual Compound – Open
Medals: Beijing 2008 Paralympic Games Individual Compound gold; 2007 World Championships 2 golds; 2010 Commonwealth Games 1 gold

Inspiration: A chance conversation on her school bus led Danielle to a local archery club. Her parents bought her a beginner's course for her 15th birthday.

Magic moment: Hitting six maximum scores to come out on top at the Beijing 2008 Games.

London 2012 target: To enjoy the experience of competing in front of a home crowd and win gold again in her own event, the Individual Compound – Open.

Need to know: In 2010, she competed against non-disabled athletes at the Commonwealth Games in Delhi, winning gold in the process. She also has a degree in Law but now trains full-time for London 2012.

Games memory: Watching the spectacular Opening Ceremony in Beijing. Danielle says it was the most amazing thing she has ever seen.

'I can't think of anything better than being a part of a Paralympics in front of your home crowd and I hope they can cheer me on to gold.'

Jessica Ennis
Athletics

TEAM GB

Born: 28 January 1986 in Sheffield
Height: 1.65m (5ft 5in)
Weight: 57kg (130lb)
Event: Heptathlon
Medals: 2009 World Championships Heptathlon gold;
2011 World Championships Heptathlon silver;
2010 European Championships 1 gold;
2006 Commonwealth Games 1 bronze

Inspiration: Watching British athlete Denise Lewis win Heptathlon gold at the Sydney 2000 Games.

Magic moment: The joy of becoming World Champion in 2009 after leading the Heptathlon from start to finish.

London 2012 target: To win Olympic gold in the Heptathlon – nothing less will do for this great athlete!

Need to know: The Heptathlon has seven events and the 100m hurdles and the high jump are Jessica's strongest. Her nickname is 'tadpole' because she is one of the smallest competitors in the Heptathlon.

Games memory: Jessica had the heartache of missing out on the Beijing 2008 Games because of a foot injury.

'Never let bad days get on top of you as a good one is around the corner.'

Mo Farah
Athletics

TEAM GB

Born: 23 March 1983 in Mogadishu, Somalia
Height: 1.75m (5ft 9in)
Weight: 65kg (140lb)
Events: 5000m and 10,000m
Medals: 2011 World Championships 5000m gold and 10,000m silver;
2006 and 2010 European Championships 2 golds and 1 silver

Inspiration: Mo's favourite sport was football but his PE teacher persuaded him to try cross country running instead. He never looked back and is now a track star.

Magic moment: Winning gold in the 5000m at the 2011 World Championships.

London 2012 target: Mo is one of the best runners in the world and is hoping for medals in his two events, the 5000m and 10,000m.

Need to know: Mo was born in Somalia and only came to the UK at the age of eight. Then in 2010 he moved to America to train. He also trains in the mountains in Kenya and the French Alps – a favourite with other Team GB athletes including Marathon star Paula Radcliffe.

Games memory: Mo ran at Beijing 2008 but didn't make it to the final of the 5000m. But in June 2011 he set a new British and European 10,000m record – his form for London 2012 looks good!

'I feel like the same person but, to be honest, as an athlete I'm a lot stronger, feel more confident and it's nice to have that.'

Dai Greene
Athletics

Born: 11 April 1986 in Llanelli, Wales
Height: 1.85m (6ft 1in)
Weight: 77kg (170lb)
Event: 400m Hurdles
Medals: 2009 World Championships 4 x 400m Relay silver; 2011 World Championships 400m Hurdles gold; 2010 European Championships 1 gold; 2010 Commonwealth Games 1 gold

'I don't shy away from the tough sessions and I am in the best shape of my life as a result.'

Inspiration: Dai dreamed of following in the footsteps of footballer and fellow Welshman Ryan Giggs and was offered a contract with Swansea City football Club, but ended up choosing Athletics instead.

Magic moment: Becoming World Champion for the first time in 2011 after running the perfect race in Daegu, South Korea.

London 2012 target: To keep doing well, break the British record and go on to take home a medal from London 2012 in the 400m Hurdles.

Need to know: Dai is right-footed but used to play football using only his left foot in an attempt to copy Giggs. Dai believes that using his 'weaker' foot a lot made him a better hurdler!

Games memory: Injury meant Dai couldn't go to Beijing 2008 – so roll on 2012!

Phillips Idowu
Athletics

TEAM GB

Born:	30 December 1978 in London
Height:	1.97m (6ft 5in)
Weight:	87kg (192lb)
Event:	Triple Jump
Medals:	Beijing 2008 Olympic Games Triple Jump silver; 2009 and 2011 World Championships 1 gold and 1 silver; 2010 European Championships 1 gold; 2002 and 2006 Commonwealth Games 1 gold and 1 silver

Inspiration: Phillips was more concerned with playing basketball and American football as a kid. But when he was 12, a PE teacher convinced him to try the Triple Jump and he's never looked back.

Magic moment: Beating the reigning Olympic Champion into second place to win the 2009 World Championships in Berlin. Phillips was presented with his winner's medal by former Triple Jump Olympic gold medallist Jonathan Edwards.

London 2012 target: Going for gold in his home city – he won't settle for less!

Need to know: Phillips' brightly dyed hair and lots of piercings make him an easy figure to spot on the athletics field. Who knows what colour his hair will be at London 2012?

Games memory: Coming very close to Olympic gold at the Beijing 2008 Games. Phillips' longest jump was only 5cm (about 2in) shorter than the winner's leap so he had to make do with silver – still a great result.

'I want to be the greatest triple jumper in the world and whatever it takes to get there, that's what I am working towards.'

David Weir
Paralympic Athletics

ParalympicsGB

Born: 5 June 1979 in London
Events: 400m, 800m and 1500m (T54 category)
Medals: Athens 2004 Paralympic Games 100m silver and 200m bronze; Beijing 2008 Paralympic Games 800m gold, 1500m gold, 400m silver and 5000m bronze; 2006 and 2011 World Championships 6 golds and 1 silver

Inspiration: Watching Paralympic Athletics legend Tanni Grey-Thompson win four gold medals at Sydney 2000 left David in tears at home in the UK, vowing to follow in her footsteps.

Magic moment: Crossing the line to win the London Marathon for a record fifth time in 2011.

London 2012 target: To win the 800m and 1500m Paralympic gold medals again. He may also compete in the 5000m and the Marathon!

Need to know: From an early age David was interested in sport – 'the more fast and furious the better' he said. He holds the British record at all track distances up to 5000m, as well as on the road at 10km, half marathon and marathon.

Games memory: David's first Paralympic medals came at Athens 2004. He won a silver and a bronze and came home determined to go one better next time around. At Beijing 2008 he did just that!

'It's going to be unbelievable – 80,000 people screaming and shouting because you are a Team GB athlete.'

Richard Whitehead
Paralympic Athletics

ParalympicsGB

Born: 19 July 1976 in Nottingham
Event: 200m (T42 category)
Medals: 2011 World Championships 200m gold

Inspiration: Richard was inspired by hearing the story of Terry Fox, an amputee who in 1980 tried to run 5,000 miles across Canada for charity. Fox called this run the 'Marathon of Hope'.

Magic moment: Winning 200m gold at the World Championships in 2011. He set a championship record in the process.

London 2012 target: To win Paralympic gold in the 200m. Richard is one of the favourites.

Need to know: Richard runs on hi-tech carbon fibre legs called blades. As well as being a sprinter, he is also a world-class long-distance runner. In 2010 he completed the Chicago marathon in 2 hours and 42 minutes – the fastest-ever time in his race category.

Games memory: 2012 will be Richard's first time at a summer Paralympic Games but he was a member of the ParalympicsGB Sledge Hockey team at the Turin 2006 Winter Games in Italy.

'Preparation is the key to success. Make sure no stone is left unturned during your preparation – then, when you're at the start line, you'll have every chance to succeed.'

Jodie Williams
Athletics

TEAM GB

Born: 28 September 1993 in Welwyn Garden City, Hertfordshire

Height: 1.74m (5ft 8½in)

Weight: 60kg (130lb)

Event: 100m

Medals: 2010 World Junior Championships 100m gold and 200m silver; 2011 European Junior Championships 2 golds and 1 bronze; 2009 World Youth Championships 2 golds

> 'I don't want to be another junior who fizzled out too soon. I want to be the name that breaks through.'

Inspiration: Both Jodie's parents were talented sprinters. Her father ran for Hertfordshire while her mother ran for Sussex. Jodie is also a sprinter and runs 100m and 200m.

Magic moment: Winning both the 100m and 200m titles at the 2011 European Junior Championships in Tallinn, Estonia. Jodie was the first British woman to complete this sprint double.

London 2012 target: To enjoy the experience of competing in such a big event. Jodie will only be 18 when London 2012 comes around.

Need to know: Between 2005 and 2010, Jodie won all 151 races she entered! She was just 100th of a second away from claiming bronze in the 60m race on her senior debut at the 2011 European Indoor Championships. In 2012, Jodie is aiming to take her A-Level exams as well as compete in the Olympic Games!

Games memory: She hasn't competed yet at an Olympic Games – watch her go!

Mark Cavendish
Cycling – Road Race

TEAM GB

Born: 21 May 1985 in Douglas, Isle of Man
Height: 1.75m (5ft 9in)
Weight: 69kg (150lb)
Event: Road Race
Medals: Road: 2011 Road World Championships gold;
2011 Tour de France Green Jersey winner;
2008–11 Tour de France 20 stage wins.
Track: 2005 and 2008 World Championships
Madison 2 golds

Inspiration: Mark started racing BMX bikes at the National Sports Centre on the Isle of Man. He got his first mountain bike at the age of 13 and started to show his talent.

Magic moment: Becoming the first-ever British rider to win the Green Jersey at the 2011 Tour de France – this colour jersey is awarded to the race's best sprinter.

London 2012 target: To win the Road Race – a 250km (155-mile) course that starts and finishes on The Mall in London.

Need to know: Mark just can't stop sprinting to victory in every race he enters all around the world. In August 2011, 200,000 spectators watched him win the London–Surrey Cycle Classic Road Race test event – a taster for 2012.

Games memory: Beijing 2008 was tough. Paired with Bradley Wiggins in the Madison, he came home without a medal – he's not used to losing!

'I'm an old-school sprinter. I can't climb a mountain but if I am in front with 200 metres to go then there's nobody who can beat me.'

Chris Hoy
Cycling – Track

TEAM GB

Born: 23 March 1976 in Edinburgh
Height: 1.85m (6ft 1in)
Weight: 92kg (200lb)
Events: Keirin, Sprint and Team Sprint
Medals: Sydney 2000 Olympic Games Team Sprint silver; Athens 2004 Olympic Games 1km Time Trial gold; Beijing 2008 Olympic Games Keirin gold, Sprint gold, Team Sprint gold; 2002–2011 World Championships 10 golds, 6 silvers and 7 bronzes; 2010 European Championships 1 bronze; 2002–2006 Commonwealth Games 2 golds and 2 bronzes

'For me London is the big one and I aim to be the best I've ever been and repeat what I did in Beijing.'

Inspiration: As a kid, Chris watched the BMX stunts in the film *E.T.* and loved them.

Magic moment: Receiving his knighthood from the Queen after becoming the first British athlete in 100 years to win three gold medals at a single Olympic Games.

London 2012 target: To win another three gold medals in the Keirin, Sprint and Team Sprint races, which would make him the most successful British Olympian ever.

Need to know: Chris is one of best athletes of all time in any sport as his vast number of medals shows! To honour him, the velodrome in Glasgow will be named after Chris, ready for the 2014 Commonwealth Games.

Games memory: Standing on top of the podium for the third time at the end of a perfect Beijing 2008 Games.

Victoria Pendleton
Cycling – Track

Born: 24 September 1980 in Stotfold, Bedfordshire
Height: 1.65m (5ft 5in)
Weight: 62kg (140lb)
Events: Sprint, Team Sprint, Keirin
Medals: Beijing 2008 Olympic Games Sprint gold;
2005–2011 World Championships 8 golds,
5 silvers and 2 bronzes; 2010–2011
European Championships 2 golds and
1 silver; 2006 Commonwealth Games
1 gold and 1 silver

'It really is all about believing in yourself: 80 per cent mental, 20 per cent physical.'

Inspiration: Watching track cyclist Jason Queally's surprise gold medal win at the Sydney 2000 Games encouraged Victoria.

Magic moment: Competing in just one event at Beijing 2008, Victoria was still waiting for her race to start as other Team GB cyclists collected their medals. With just one shot at Olympic glory she comfortably won gold.

London 2012 target: Another gold in the Sprint race, plus medals in the Team Sprint and Keirin, then retire!

Need to know: Victoria started racing on grass tracks when she was just nine years old. She can train for up to eight hours a day!

Games memory: After finishing ninth in the Sprint and sixth in the 500m Time Trial at Athens 2004 Victoria thought about quitting. But she bounced back with a brilliant gold at Beijing 2008.

Shanaze Reade
Cycling – BMX

TEAM GB

Born: 23 September 1988 in Crewe, Cheshire
Height: 1.72m (5ft 8in)
Weight: 76kg (170lb)
Event: BMX
Medals: BMX: 2007, 2008 and 2010 World Championships gold. Track: 2007 and 2008 World Championships Team Sprint gold; 2009 World Championships Team Sprint silver

Inspiration: Shanaze was a talented athlete and looked up to track star Kelly Holmes. But at the age of 10 she started riding a BMX and by the time she was 13 she was the British senior champion!

Magic moment: Each of her three BMX World Championship victories was special.

London 2012 target: Having won the 2011 BMX Supercross World Cup event at the new Olympic Park track, Shanaze is hunting for gold again.

Need to know: When BMX racing became an Olympic sport Shanaze started training with the GB Track Cycling squad. She was paired with Victoria Pendleton in the Team Sprint event. Just one month after Shanaze's first-ever track race she was a World Champion! So, Shanaze could compete in the Team Sprint again in 2012 as well as in BMX.

Games memory: The heartache of crashing out of the Beijing 2008 BMX final after being gold medal favourite. Roll on 2012 to put things right!

'The BMX Track looks absolutely amazing. I think it will definitely be exciting racing.'

Sarah Storey
Paralympic Cycling

ParalympicsGB

Born: 26 October 1977 in Manchester

Events: Individual Time Trial and Individual Pursuit (LC1-2/CP4 category)

Medals: Cycling: Beijing 2008 Paralympic Games Individual Time Trial and Individual Pursuit gold; 2006–2007 World Championships 2 golds, 2 silvers and 2 bronzes; 2005 European Championships 3 golds, 1 silver. Swimming: 1992–2004 Paralympic Games 5 golds, 8 silvers and 3 bronzes

Inspiration: Aged just six years old, Sarah saw British swimmer Sarah Hardcastle win silver and bronze at the Los Angeles 1984 Olympic Games.

Magic moment: Winning six Swimming medals aged just 14 at the Barcelona 1992 Paralympic Games.

London 2012 target: To win her two races again. She may also earn a place in the Olympic Games women's Team Pursuit, which would make her the first British athlete to compete in both the Paralympic and Olympic Games!

Need to know: Sarah is one of Great Britain's greatest athletes. She first spent 13 years as a swimmer, winning 16 Paralympic medals, and only started Cycling in 2005 after an ear infection kept her out of the pool.

Games memory: Sarah says, 'Every time I'm on top of the rostrum with the GB suit on and the anthem is playing it is special.'

'You work all the time to be the best, and when you end up being the best in the world, it's just amazing. Every time is just like the first.'

Tom Daley
Aquatics – Diving

TEAM GB

Born: 21 May 1994 in Plymouth
Height: 1.80m (5ft 9in)
Weight: 59kg (130lb)
Events: 10m Platform and Synchronised 10m Platform
Medals: 2009 World Championships Individual 10m Platform gold; 2008 European Championships 1 gold; 2010 Commonwealth Games 2 golds

'There are so many sacrifices, you have to train so hard and when you come out on top of the world it's crazy.'

Inspiration: Tom started out aged seven at a diving club in Plymouth. One of his childhood heroes was Leon Taylor, who won silver at Athens 2004.

Magic moment: Performing the second perfect dive of his career when it mattered – scoring 10 from all seven judges – to win the Individual 10m Platform competition at the 2010 Commonwealth Games.

London 2012 target: To match the gold medal he won at the 2009 World Championships in his two Olympic events – the 10m Platform and the Synchronised 10m Platform.

Need to know: He has never been beaten in his age group at any National championship event. As well as training for London 2012, Tom is also preparing to take his A-Levels.

Games memory: Tom was just 14 when he went to the Beijing 2008 Games, where he was the youngest member of Team GB since 1960. He made it to the final in both his events.

Lee Pearson
Paralympic Equestrian

ParalympicsGB

Born: 4 February 1974 in Cheddleton, Staffordshire

Events: Championships Test (Grade 1b), Freestyle Test (Grade 1b), Team (Grade 1a)

Medals: Sydney 2000, Athens 2004 and Beijing 2008 Paralympic Games Championships Test gold, Freestyle Test gold, Team gold; 1999–2010 World and European Championships 18 golds and 1 silver

'I don't think the general public knows what's going to hit them. It's huge. I've been to the last three Paralympic Games and know the impact they have.'

Inspiration: Watching the Atlanta 1996 Games on television made Lee think he could do it himself. He did.

Magic moment: Lee is the only disabled athlete to have won a title at the British National Dressage Championships, usually won by a non-disabled rider. He came first in 2003.

London 2012 target: Lee has won gold in every event he has entered since Sydney 2000 – winning nine golds so far! He is aiming to win the Championships Test, Freestyle Test (both Grade 1a) and Team – Open events again in 2012.

Need to know: Lee is the most successful Paralympic rider of all time and now competes on a horse named Gentleman. His first mount was a donkey called Sally!

Games memory: The Sydney 2000 Paralympic Games, where finishing with three golds was just incredible.

Richard Kruse
Fencing

Born: 30 July 1983 in London
Height: 1.90m (6ft 3in)
Weight: 82kg (181lb)
Events: Individual Foil and Team Foil
Medals: 2009 European Championships Individual Foil silver;
2009–2011 World Cup 1 gold and 2 silvers

Inspiration: It is Richard's mum who can take the credit for introducing him to Fencing. He was just 10 when she took him to a local club for lessons.

Magic moment: Winning a silver medal in the Foil event at the 2011 World Cup in Seoul, South Korea. Richard lost the final by just one point but showed off his great talent.

London 2012 target: Richard is Team GB's best hope of a Fencing medal in the Individual Foil competition. He also hopes to lead the Team Foil.

Need to know: Away from Fencing, Richard practises a form of Kung Fu as part of his strength training.

Games memory: Finishing in eighth place at Athens 2004. It was the best result by any British fencer at the Olympic Games since Tokyo 1964.

'The two Olympic Games (Athens 2004 and Beijing 2008) have been by far the best tournaments I've competed in to date.'

Louis Smith
Gymnastics

Born: 22 April 1989 in Peterborough, Cambridgeshire
Height: 1.79m (5ft 10in)
Weight: 76kg (168lb)
Events: All Artistic Gymnastics events, expert in Pommel Horse
Medals: Beijing 2008 Olympic Games Pommel Horse bronze; 2007–2011 World Championships 1 silver and 2 bronzes; 2009–2010 European Championships 3 silvers; 2006 Commonwealth Games 1 gold and 1 bronze

Inspiration: Louis was just four years old when he started gymnastics lessons, following his elder brother.

Magic moment: Winning the Junior European Pommel Horse title in 2004. Louis realised that he could be a senior champion.

London 2012 target: To move up to the silver or gold position.

Need to know: There are six elements in men's Gymnastics and Louis takes part in them all but excels at the Pommel Horse. He claims that his long arms are the secret of his success.

Games memory: Winning bronze at Beijing 2008 – the first British gymnast to win an individual Olympic medal since London 1908!

'I am trying to fulfil my dream ... I am going to be pushing for a gold medal.'

Beth Tweddle
Gymnastics

Born: 1 April 1985 in Johannesburg, South Africa

Height: 1.61m (5ft 3in)

Weight: 53kg (120lb)

Events: All Artistic Gymnastics events, expert in Floor and Uneven Bars

Medals: 2003 and 2005 World Championships Uneven Bars bronze, 2006 World Championships Uneven Bars gold; 2009 World Championships Floor gold; 2002–2011 European Championships 6 golds, 5 silvers and 1 bronze; 2002 Commonwealth Games 1 gold and 2 silvers

'Everyone keeps telling me how old I am but the motivation is there and that's London 2012.'

Inspiration: Beth tried lots of different sports, including ballet, horse riding and swimming, before her mum took her to a gymnastics club.

Magic moment: Winning the gold medal in the Floor competition at the 2009 World Championships in London.

London 2012 target: To win an Olympic medal to go with all her other titles. London 2012 will be her last competition and it would be great to retire on a high.

Need to know: There are four elements in women's Gymnastic and Beth competes in them all. However, she's best at the Floor and Uneven Bars events. Beth is also known as the greatest British gymnast ever.

Games memory: Agonisingly missing out on a medal by 0.25 points in the Uneven Bars at Beijing 2008.

Tom Aggar
Paralympic Rowing

Born: 24 May 1984 in London

Event: Single Sculls (ASMx1 category)

Medals: Beijing 2008 Paralympic Games Single Sculls gold; 2007–2011 World Championships 4 golds

Inspiration: **It was clear Tom had real talent when he won the British Indoor Rowing championships in 2006. The following year he began to row outdoors on water.**

Magic moment: **Leading from start to finish to win gold at Beijing 2008.**

London 2012 target: **To win another gold in his event, the Single Sculls – ASMx1. It's looking good – Tom has never lost a race in international competition.**

Need to know: **His upper body strength and long arms have helped make him a Paralympic champion and he even beat his own world record for the sixth time in 2009!**

Games memory: **Rowing made its first appearance at the Beijing 2008 Paralympic Games and becoming the first men's champion in the Single Sculls is something Tom will never forget.**

'I love that I'm on my own, it's all down to me!'

Katherine Grainger and Anna Watkins

Rowing

TEAM GB

Born: Katherine: 12 November 1975 in Glasgow; Anna: 13 February 1983 in Leek, Staffordshire

Height: Katherine: 1.82m (5ft 11in); Anna: 1.83m (6ft 0in)

Weight: Katherine: 80kg (176lb); Anna: 79kg (174lb)

Event: Double Sculls (2x)

Medals won together: 2010 and 2011 World Championships Double Sculls gold

Inspiration: Both took up rowing at university – Katherine at Edinburgh, Anna at Cambridge. Their coaches told them to aim high.

Magic moment: Their win in the 2011 World Championships confirmed that they are still ahead of their rivals.

London 2012 target: Nobody has beaten them since they started rowing together and both already have Olympic Games experience. So gold is a real possibility.

Need to know: Katherine is the best British female rower ever. She has three Olympic silver medals and is a six-time World Champion. Anna won bronze at Beijing 2008 and is a two-time World Champion.

Games memories: Katherine came close to gold at Beijing 2008 in the Quadruple Sculls event, while Anna won bronze with a different partner in the Double Sculls.

Katherine says: 'The way we row and the way we are together is very, very special.'

Zac Purchase and Mark Hunter
Rowing

TEAM GB

Born: Zac: 2 May 1986 in Cheltenham, Gloucestershire;
Mark: 1 July 1978 in London

Height: Zac: 1.86m (6ft 1in); Mark: 1.83m (6ft 0in)

Weight: Both men weigh 70kg (154lb)

Event: Lightweight Double Sculls (2x)

Medals won together: Beijing 2008 Olympic Games Lightweight Double Sculls gold; 2007–11 World Championships 1 gold and 2 bronzes

Inspiration: Zac loved rowing at school. Mark grew up in east London – just over a mile away from the London 2012 Olympic Stadium.

Magic moment: Winning gold in Olympic record time at Beijing 2008.

London 2012 target: Zac and Mark are the duo to beat for gold, especially as they won their Lightweight Double Sculls race again at the World Championships last year.

Need to know: As a youngster, Zac was too small to row and had to be a cox until he got older. After Beijing 2008, Mark retired but made a comeback.

Games memory: After Beijing 2008, Mark said 'I've been dying for this day since I started rowing.'

Mark says: 'We trust and believe in each other.'

Ben Ainslie
Sailing

Born: 5 February 1977 in Macclesfield, Cheshire
Height: 1.83m (6ft 0in)
Weight: 90kg (198lb)
Event: Finn (one-person dinghy (heavyweight))
Medals: Atlanta 1996 Olympic Games Laser silver; Sydney 2000 Olympic Games Laser gold; Athens 2004 and Beijing 2008 Olympic Games Finn gold; 1993–2010 World Championships 10 golds; 1993–2008 European Championships 9 golds

'Just competing in 2012 would be a once-in-a-lifetime opportunity for everyone involved on home waters.'

Inspiration: His father, Roddy, was Ben's inspiration. Roddy was skipper of a boat that took part in the Round the World yacht race in 1973 and 1974.

Magic moment: Beating star Brazilian sailor Robert Scheidt to win gold at the Sydney 2000 Games.

London 2012 target: It has to be another gold medal. If he achieves this Ben will equal Danish sailor Paul Elvstrom's record of four golds.

Need to know: Ben started sailing in Cornwall when he was eight and won his first world title when he was only 16. Before Athens 2004, Ben put on 18kg (40lb) of muscle as he moved up to the Finn class event. Finn boats are big and he needed the extra strength to compete. Ben is also the only sailor to be crowned World Sailor of the Year three times.

Games memory: Winning his third Olympic gold at Beijing 2008. It was a special victory because Ben had been ill before the competition started.

Rebecca Adlington
Aquatics – Swimming

TEAM GB

Born: 17 February 1989 in Mansfield, Nottinghamshire

Height: 1.79m (5ft 9in)

Weight: 70kg (154lb)

Events: 800m and 400m Freestyle

Medals: Beijing 2008 Olympic Games 400m and 800m Freestyle gold; 2008–2011 World Championships 2 golds, 2 silvers and 2 bronzes; 2006 and 2010 European Championships 1 gold, 1 silver and 1 bronze; 2010 Commonwealth Games 2 golds and 2 bronzes

'You have to get up at five in the morning but if you didn't do the hard work you wouldn't succeed.'

Inspiration: Winning two silver medals at the Youth Olympic Games when she was 14 gave Rebecca the belief that she could succeed as a swimmer.

Magic moment: Touching the wall just 0.07 seconds before her American rival Katie Hoff to win her first Olympic gold in the 400m Freestyle.

London 2012 target: To win again in both her Olympic races as part of a great Team GB squad.

Need to know: Rebecca's races are the 400m and 800m Freestyle. In winning her second Olympic gold, she set a new world record - knocking a massive 2.12 seconds off the previous best time. Rebecca has worked with her coach, Bill Furniss, since she was 12 years old. The pool in Mansfield where she learned to swim was renamed The Rebecca Adlington Swimming Centre in her honour.

Games memory: Standing on the rostrum with teammate and bronze medal winner Joanne Jackson after the 400m Freestyle final at Beijing 2008.

Keri-Anne Payne
Aquatics – Swimming

Born: 9 December 1987 in Johannesburg, South Africa

Height: 1.75m (5ft 9in)

Weight: 67kg (148lb)

Event: 10km Marathon

Medals: Beijing 2008 Olympic Games 10km Marathon silver; 2009 and 2011 World Championships 10km Open Water gold; 2004 European Championships 400m Freestyle bronze; 2010 Commonwealth Games 400m Individual Medley bronze

'To be on that Olympic team at a home Olympics is going to be absolutely amazing.'

Inspiration: Keri-Anne followed her elder brother and sister into the pool. Further inspiration came from the achievements of Olympic bronze medallist Steve Parry who, like Keri-Anne, trained at the Stockport Metro Swimming Club.

Magic moment: The 2007 World Championships in Melbourne was unusual – the water was full of jellyfish!

London 2012 target: The 10km Marathon race – Keri-Anne's best event – will take place in the Serpentine lake in Hyde Park. The race lasts six laps and at the end, Keri-Anne will hopefully be in first place.

Need to know: When she won the 2011 World Championships, Keri-Anne became the first athlete from any sport to qualify to represent Team GB at London 2012.

Games memory: Winning the silver medal at Beijing 2008. It was the first time the 10km Marathon race had been part of the Olympic programme.

Ellie Simmonds
Paralympic Swimming

ParalympicsGB

Born: 11 November 1994 in Walsall, West Midlands

Events: 100m and 400m Freestyle, 200m Backstroke, 4 x 100m Freestyle Relay and Medley Relay (S6 category)

Medals: Beijing 2008 Paralympic Games 100m and 400m Freestyle gold; 2009 and 2010 World Championships 8 golds, 5 silvers and 1 bronze; 2009–2011 European Championships 5 golds, 2 silvers and 2 bronzes

'You train so hard and when I achieved my goals, all the emotion came out.'

Inspiration: Ellie saw the Swimming competition at the Athens 2004 Paralympic Games and thought, 'I could do that.'

Magic moment: At Beijing 2008 Ellie did not know she had won the 100m Freestyle race until she looked up at the scoreboard. The shock on her face was clear for all to see.

London 2012 target: To try and win the 100m and 400m Freestyle events again and aim for medals in the 200m Backstroke, 4 x 100m Freestyle Relay and Medley Relay events.

Need to know: Ellie and her mum moved from Walsall to Wales so Ellie could train at the Swansea Performance club. Ellie holds three separate World Records – in the 100m and 400m Freestyle and 200m Individual Medley.

Games memory: Ellie thought that everything about Beijing 2008 was spectacular. She just wished she had time to experience more of it.

Sarah Stevenson
Taekwondo

Born: 30 March 1983 in Doncaster, North Yorkshire
Height: 1.77m (5ft 10in)
Weight: 72kg (159lb)
Event: Over 67kg
Medals: Beijing 2008 Olympic Games Over 67kg bronze; 2001 and 2011 World Championships gold; 2005 World Championships 1 silver; 2002–2010 European Championships 4 golds and 2 silvers

'I can win gold. I'm World Champion. I just want it to happen on that day and I'm going to do my best to make sure it does.'

Inspiration: Sarah's older brother Simon was a junior Taekwondo international. Sarah followed and became Britain's first-ever Taekwondo World Champion.

Magic moment: Becoming World Champion for the second time in May 2011.

London 2012 target: With home support, Sarah will hope for a medal.

Need to know: Sarah's bronze medal at Beijing 2008 was Team GB's first-ever Olympic Taekwondo medal. London 2012 will be Sarah's fourth Olympic Games.

Games memory: Sarah actually lost her quarter-final at Beijing 2008 but the judges looked again at their scoring decisions and declared her the winner! She had just 20 minutes to get ready for the semi-final.

Alistair Brownlee
Triathlon

TEAM GB

Born: 23 April 1988 in Dewsbury, Yorkshire
Height: 1.84cm (6ft 0in)
Weight: 70kg (154lb)
Event: Triathlon
Medals: 2009 and 2011 World Triathlon Championships gold; 2009 and 2011 European Triathlon Championships gold

'Going out to win is the best policy.'

Inspiration: Alistair comes from a sporting family. His father was a runner, his mother was a swimmer and his uncle introduced him to triathlon.

Magic moment: Winning the World Championship Series event on the Olympic Triathlon course in Hyde Park in August 2011. It put Alistair top of the world rankings.

London 2012 target: To win Team GB's first-ever Triathlon gold.

Need to know: Triathlon combines swimming, running and cycling. Alistair's younger brother Jonny is also an international standard triathlete. The brothers live and train together and will both be contenders at London 2012. Alistair also has a degree in Physiology and Sport.

Games memory: Beijing 2008 proved to be a great experience for Alistair. Aged just 20 he was the second-youngest athlete in the event and finished 12th overall.

Andrew Lapthorne and Peter Norfolk
Wheelchair Tennis

ParalympicsGB

Born: Andrew: 11 October 1990 in Middlesex; Peter: 13 December 1960 in London

Event: Doubles – Quad

Titles won together: 2011 Australian Open champions; 2011 Super Series in St Louis champions

Inspiration: Andrew started playing aged 13 when he attended a Tennis Foundation Wheelchair Tennis camp. Peter only started playing the game when he was 30 – the same year that Andrew was born!

Magic moment: Winning their first Grand Slam as a Doubles pairing at the 2011 Australian Open.

London 2012 target: Andrew and Peter will go into the Games as the highest ranked doubles partnership in the world. They will face serious competition from American rivals Nick Taylor and David Wagner.

Need to know: It will be Andrew's first Paralympic Games but Peter's third – he's already won two golds, one silver and one bronze medal.

Games memory: What Peter remembers most of all is the relief of hitting the winning shots at the last two Paralympic Games.

Peter says: 'I dream of winning, I visualise the podium, and it's just amazing.'

31

Credits

TEAM GB

ParalympicsGB

The publishers would like to thank the following sources for their kind permission to reproduce the pictures in this book. The page numbers for each of the photographs are listed below, giving the page on which they appear in the book and any location indicator (T-top, B-bottom, L-left, R-right)

Action Images: /Mark Blinch/Reuters: 3BL, 6; /Adam Holt: 3TL, 10; /Jason Lee/ Reuters: 16; /Jason O'Brien: 8, 32TL; /Nigel Roddis/Reuters: 12; /Aly Song/ Reuters: 24; /Bobby Yip/Reuters: 18, 32BL

Getty Images: /Clive Brunskill: 21; /China Photos: 31L; / ChinaFotoPress: 2, 17; /Julian Finney: 31R; /Cate Gillon: 28; /Jed Jacobsohn: 20; /Nick Laham: 27; /Feng Li: 22; /Clive Mason: 25, 32BR; /Jamie McDonald: 19; /Chris McGrath: 7; / Sandra Mu: 23; /Gary M Prior: 15; /Quinn Rooney: 3BR, 13; / Javier Soriano/AFP: 5; /Jamie Squire: 26; /Chris Trotman: 11; / Andrew Wong: 4

Press Association Images: /John Giles: 14; /John Walton: 30; /Andy Wong/AP: 9; /Zou Zheng/Landov: 29

Every effort has been made to acknowledge correctly and contact the source and/or copyright holder of each picture and Carlton Books Limited apologises for any unintentional errors or omissions that will be corrected in future editions of this book.